Kimble Psalms

Prayer of a Psalmist

Anthony T. Kimble

WestBow
P R E S S
A DIVISION OF THOMAS NELSON

WestBow Press books may be ordered through booksellers or by contacting:

WestBow Press
A Division of Thomas Nelson
1663 Liberty Drive
Bloomington, IN 47403
www.westbowpress.com
1-(866) 928-1240

ISBN: 978-1-4497-0411-7 (sc)
ISBN: 978-1-4497-0456-8 (e)

Library of Congress Control Number: 2010933030

Printed in the United States of America

WestBow Press rev. date: 7/21/2010

How could just one man alone make a difference in a world filled with hate, crime, and animosity? Am I not only human, am I just another person with the same intentions at hand as well as my fellow brother. For God alone made water, trees, and sand that blows along the beaches and throughout the great lands of this country. God made man in his own image which makes the likes of my being powerful in the eye of my enemy. For with everyday trials that stand tall against me, it is the blood and of generations before my time inheritance in which make me strong; can I do all things through Christ without the knowledge of knowing him? Can I follow in my great ancestors footsteps and smite the coming of my enemies? Who am I to judge who or what I should be, no man can correct his own destiny if it is already written. I have not sold my soul nor am I to lose it.

God brings as much as needed out of me and spare the rest to the unbelievers. My prayers are only citations without faith; hope will only last for so long until tiring out. If I last until morning I would not have to give in, just rest my mind until then. Let faith cover me like a warm blanket and stand guard against the unwanted. God please don't be alarmed by my absentmindedness and lack of faith, for I may rest now to regain my strength. Give me the means to complete your will so that I may forbear, a promising future. I may not last but keep me satisfied with the milk and meat of your words and life. Grab my hand and sketch the implements of success. Lord please here me, I need your help and guidance today.

The Lamb of God

YOU ARE GOOD

Lord I lift my hands and extend all of my praises unto you, praising you and exalting your mighty name. You show mercy and affection towards me, for your will may lay flat in my hands to surely pass over. I hide my face behind the walls of your cross, not to be cowardly characterized but to be put to rest along with you; my savior. I will not fall short until it has come to pass and all efforts have been exhausted. King of Kings, the bread of life; take my word Lord and never lay me down. Let the rocks cry out and the trees stretch their branches and the wind whisper. Let the seasons take action and prepare a welcoming for you all mighty.

I set a table for the just as well as the unjust, to dine with me, to laugh with me, and speak of your goodness Lord. Give them the guidance and restoration bestowed in me, let the church sing a new song for today is good. The Sabbath is holy and I praise you lord for it even the more. Oh God understand me when I say halleluiah...halleluiah.... halleluiah for the lord my God has been good. Even as I bed down, I praise in sleep; when I wake up, I praise in with a yawn; and when I walk among others my mouth shall be a faucet to those who thirst. I shall never go without praise in my spirit; temptation will corrupt my soul and lead me to the front door of failure. Take my cloths and sandals to be washed along with me. For my enemy is clueless of what is yet to come; the scent of your blood is pure and cause them to divert from me. Thank you Lord for salvation and freedom from sin and unrighteousness, the key has been sealed away within the walls of glory, the structure from which you live and breathe. Hear my cry and accept my prayer. Deal with me on a level fit for your doers and just. Give the unjust a definition to all who do not understand them and all who oppose them. Break my bone to use as a rod for the wicked and a weapon for the evil present in this place.

Father call out to me so that I may be able to approach you; beat on my drum to awaken the dancing spirit that has been kept in captivity. I have a purpose with only praise and worship, nothing more. The skies have fallen deep for me now for today I may search for you and for tomorrow I will have found what I have been looking for. Let the surface be a blessing to those who come near the things that I touch. Let my words be a tunnel for all to venture; teach and guide them never to get lost. Lord, like sweet honey your blood covers me; let me drink from your cup and never fill ashamed. Father, my Lord of this earth; break all of my ways that are unpleasant to your expectations. Punish me with the pain of understanding and not in vain; pierce my side with the spear of righteousness. Unlock the Holy Spirit and never detain it, let me dance in peace and not be ashamed. Break the old me and give the new being life through Jesus, my Lord and savior. Praises shall go up and I expect nothing in return for you have done enough, my praise is nothing more but thanksgiving. God please understand my heart, come into my home I have prepared for your presents. Anoint my walls and shield my hands from the unwelcome. Take part in my growth and journey; I am seeking you Lord, seeking perfection. I beg you almighty never let go until I close my eyes even then will I continue to seek you. I have fallen so close to you that I am able to hear your heart beat next to me. I love you God and I never intend to leave you side.

PURPOSE

Tell me, where does this road lead to? The end is unclear; vague and intense fog shields my purpose. Tails of sorrow, fear, and depression shapes my memory into an insane nature; blue skies sometimes, if nothing at all. Only the faint forms of clouds and nothing more, is there anything there? Is it just a figure of my imagination or a mirage of my insanity? God lead not the dark waters but the red sea of hope and freedom of knowing what's yet to come. Hopes of making it at least a mile up the road have dried up like the tears from my eyes, the sweat from my body. Aching bones tell me to give up it's pointless, but the spirit remains headstrong. My hands are tied behind my back and yours are stretch out towards me, I am not able to touch what is so close. Give the right way to my bones and have mercy for I am not worthy to carry such a burden; for I am only human and nothing more, created in your image and not the form of godliness.

My neighbor sits and rest beside a stone; he folds his arms and drifts away in sleep. I have falling to my hands and knees to crawl now, while he sleeps and dreams. Can't you see and understand this lord, why can't I too take up my stone and rest. Is it not good enough for you that I have chosen a savior, is it not good enough that I have chosen a side? Lifting my head, crawling in hopes to see where I am going at least for a while to get an idea. My faith has run scarce and my day of suffering has gone far enough. I drag now looking beyond my occupied space, one…two…three…four holes that are distant from each other, falling down deep into one. Deep….deep….deep I fall unable to grab on to any branches. I see your hand but still I am unable to grab on to you. Stop! There is no use now I have reached the bottom. Get away from me! I can't believe you allowed me to fall. I climb back to the top and commenced crawling, there is no time for recovery. I see the second hole and fall down deep…deep….deep. Where are you? I crawl back out myself without a hand to assist me. I am discouraged and weak, lord I cry out to you and there is no answer not even from my neighbor who remains asleep. The third hole I managed to get around but shockingly ending up at the bottom, laying on my back I refuse to move any further down this road. God had abandoned me giving favor to my neighbor who remains at rest.

I rise up and lay against the wall of the dark hole preparing myself to make yet another climb back out without assistance. Though fallen three times I came to quickly realized that God was standing at the top waiting for me. Lord you have been there all this time and yet bothered to assist me, for what purpose I do not understand. Your love for me seems to have faded, why? Have I not been loyal and consistent? It is I your servant who sustained expectations and yet you leave me. Take pride in me as I take pride and honor in you lord. Lead me not into temptation but victory; I am willing to follow you even into death. Yet you leave me alone. *Fret no more my son; yes it is I who has leaded you through these paths and harsh situations. Surely I say to you, this storm was to make you stronger and better. You've inspired your neighbor to pick up his stone and press on; you have shown*

LIFE IN YOUR PRESENTS

Lord, I am happy with what I am dealt with in life even through the bad times and addle situations. I time myself adequately and patiently keeping your words in mind; confident one day in time I will make your great words history. Feel my heart lord and take action to prevent any sudden attacks from my enemy who so desires my soul. Rap me with your divine light and precious spirit so that I may feel safe and secure. God I come knocking at your door bearing gifts of my labor neatly raped in love to give to you. Accept my kind heart and heal my broken spirit. I give to you lord everything that my name and hands touches, for you are the reason of my being. I owe my life to you and much more. Nothing shall be put in my hands before yours, with a blessing from you will I except those things.

God if I could only understand your thoughts towards me. If I only knew how you thought of me, surely I may be contempt for tonight and for tomorrow be reassured. I kiss the ground in which was created and walked by you God. Lay my head down beside the still waters and watch as your powers make it dance. I will spend eternity sitting with the trees and beside mountains only because they were touched by your hands alone. My body is treated with pride and the most high for I am created in an image of you. With my hands I heal those who you Lord so desire to be. With my heart I encourage those you appoint me to do so. With my tongue, speak only those words you ask of me and speak only those words you have spoke. Bless the unbelievers and heal the prayerful, it's their light that paves the way for many to see and understand you Lord. I will die before I am leaded into the house of the enemy. The blood that flourishes my body tells a story of transgression, abuse, purity, love, and a testimony. Scorn me for disobeying your word and dishonor my rights established by your hands Lord. I follow you Lord even in to death. Give my legs to the cripple, give these eyes to my brother, stomp on my heart so that I may understand what so many are going through; leave my infant body at the foot of a dumpster to find a new home. Lord understand me when I say; teach me to love, cherish, obey, and pray.

Teach me to love others the way I love you Lord. Let me go so that I may know how to talk to them. Give me your blessing; let me carry your cross until I am crawling with it and even the more let me die with it in my arms. I cry out to you Lord for so little and still you manage to give me more, more than I can hold in these arms. How can your heart be so bright and fluorescent and still I have hate hiding within the walls of mine. Is it impossible to reach a level such as yours and dwell beside you my Lord in your great kingdom? I am not worthy to speak of these things even to you Lord, but show me how to ride along side your great wings. Teach me not the ways of your doings but show me how to get there. I may have fallen short but will not fall deep. Lord, my love for you grows so enormous; I can't live without hearing your voice, I refuse to eat without you joining me, I will not breathe until you bless me; I can't accept this world being so distant from heaven. Take my hand Lord and I may fall to my knees in honor of finally reaching you.

TO WORSHIP YOU I LIVE

To worship you I live, to dine beside my savior and feast upon wonders not of this world. To take part in history man has not yet seen nor heard of. For it is a blessing to be here without the blood of youth but of Christ, give me not the mind of man but the character of a king. Breathe life into my wounds and heal my broken heart father. Bless those who are unable to speak of these words and heal those who can. Guide my thoughts and keep me from the sinful ways of the wicked. You have my word and my life extended out towards heaven, as I lift my hands and drop to my knees in preparation. Let the heavens rain down on me Lord and give my life meaning. Let those who oppose me know who I serve and those who stand against me understand your power, my name is victory. Bless those who love me and my words, let my word be an essential part in lives of those who approach me. To worship you I live, and to worship you I will die.

No man shall strip me of my pride and love I have for God, I take my own sword to my chest before I am held against my will. I give my neighbor his sword before he submits to the enemy with your name on his tongue. What an awesome God in me that I give to the world. To worship you father I live, through my storms I will worship, up and down mountains I shall worship, and even through the most dreadful times in my life I will worship. Take my word and stone it into tablets of glory Lord. Make my tongue of great value and worth more than gold, cleanse my life with the pure heart and mind of your awesomeness. Help me to rise above your expectations reaching unbreakable heights. To worship you I live and to worship you I will surely die.

SOLDIER OF GOD

Even before my existence I knew that I was anointed and appointed for a specific task. As a child growing up I understood that I was purposed. I would hope the reader gets a clear understanding of Gods power which flows through me and desires the same for themselves. I pray that your life will be congested and overflowing with so much glory and light. I sing unto you a song in which soothe the spirit and restores what has been wounded. Lift your hands and receive God's blessing, it doesn't matter if you're at work; let the employees witness the anointing of God. At this point you should feel his presents. Stand to your feet and lift your hands where ever you are, this is your opening. As you began to feel lighter and lighter think about how many times God brought you out of a situation into a better place. Welcome to my world, how does this feel to you? Imagine shaking all the pressure blocks off. Imagine a spring washing away all your sadness, sickness, and worries.

Now hold on to God, do not allow him to leave without a blessing or new anointing. Continue praising and worshipping God for all things including future blessings in the making. This is a good place to praise and give thanks; this is a good place for victory. The bible tells us that when praises go up blessings come down; I pray that Jesus may come down instead and heal, feel, restore, and bless you personally. It would be selfish of me to not share the same bond that I have with God, for I pray that you too may be able to hear him breathe softly in your ear, because he is so close. I pray that you too may feel his gentle hand on your shoulder, and his voice whisper to you throughout the day. Open your heart to receive this, thank God rather than pray at this moment, for it is already done. God knows all your problems and circumstances up to this point; there is no need to explain to him, just give thanks and praises unto his name. Some people who read this may have fallen deeper into these words, for their soul is thirsty and longs for God. It is a great feeling to have God resting beside you. I thank you for listening and bless you for coming thus far. Go even farther by reading this again and again until the anointing of God is surely upon you. Read this until everything you touch shall feel the power of God. Continue reading this until you are overflowing with love.

DEEP IN THE MIND OF A WORSHIPER

Deep in the mind of a worshiper, it is evident the spirit has been wounded, beaten, and betrayed. Thrown from off the horse and placed upon a pedestal fit for dogs. With very little hope and an equal amount of faith, pressing forward will be difficult. In this dark place acts of violence, animosity, and temptation feeds never getting full nor satisfied. It is inevitable; God promised some bad days but never stated the details or level of its winds. Let me drink from the fountain that shall never run dry, for if I drink of your water I may find peace. At least for only a day will suffice the feeble spirit; don't weep, just stand tall and pray for a moment. Goliath have come for me again, God I need strength; at this point given up would be better than going on.

Deep within the mind of a worshiper, blood flows more than tears; the only comfort is the soft melody of praise. All that I can do at this point is force a smile even if it hurts. Don't cry it will end soon, just hang in there. The darkness has filled my home and has caused me to flee. Another victim to this world never fighting back but standing tall, never just smile and accept this as a gift. Evidently there is great power in my future. Goliath has taken everything, including my health; broken my body and strip me of my character. I am drinking now, for it is the only way to relieve the pain. Just have this one drink and leave it alone for good, my words are promises to a little kid. It has been a while but finally, peace falls over me and I survive another night. Now that the sun rules the sky the same wind comes pushing me out the front door to settle in a puddle of sadness and depression.

Deep in the mind of a worshiper, shameful habits draws hate upon me. Being judged and harassed for what I do rather than who I am, again finding that life isn't really worth living anymore. My own mother sheds tears over my lack of ability to understand and comprehend. She talks to many others about my absentmindedness and screams at my father for his frail spirit. In the end, they both scream at each other; I hear it for the last time. One pill after another I take until finally sleep falls upon me. Death informed God and was denied my soul. Once again silence in the mind of a worshipper.

Deep in the mind of a worshiper God tells me to come bringing the Brocken wings from off my back. I slowly walk forward; it has been a while since my father called my name. Please don't be mad at me, commence taking more pills to keep from shame. Again he calls my name and with power in his voice, knocking the bottle from my hand and sending me to the ground. It is true, my Lord request me and will stop at nothing to grab my attention. I can't find my wings; they were on my back a while ago, hesitating for a second realizing the failure I am once again. God calls my name once more sending me to the floor. I answer this time slowly progressing towards the altar. *Deep in the mind of a worshiper the good separates from the evil, and the evil shall perish under the constant commitment to prayer and to God. To live and breathe by me is to live and breathe freely without sadness or depression, without sickness or diseases, without damnation. I have power over both good and evil, day and night, I am God your creator and giver of life. Take off your shoes and cast them behind you, then take off your clothes and throw them into the fire. Take the cup that is in front of you and drink until you have had your fill then douse the remaining contents at your feet. Here me when I say, your Goliath has been slain. It is time for all man to confess and bow before the true and phenomenal power of God.*

In the mind of a worshiper I have a new song; a song of peace and joy, a song worth listening to, a song that has meaning and difference, a song of prosperous life and phenomenal change. I've been redeemed and filled, covered with blood that has been spilled for my transgressions.

FOR MY LIFE

In August of 2009 I picked up the phone then made a life changing phone call to my unit In Saint Peters, Missouri. I had two options, either make something happen or waste my life away which would have resulted in death. My mother, who I was staying with at the time, didn't have much to say but I knew that my decision on going to Iraq would have a catastrophic level of stress on both her and my family, but I knew it had to be done. Faith played a major role; I recall praying and asking God for protection as I boarded the plane. At that moment I leaned back in my seat and gazed out the window admiring the scenery, it was the closes I have been to God in a while and it felt good. A voice, the most soft and peaceful voice assured me of life. I closed my eyes and drifted off to sleep, this was the start of my 13 months; 13 months that would change my life forever.

Landing in Iraq wasn't until late October, flight lasting a little over 13 hours. With boots on ground and about 170 U.S. soldiers at the time of our arrival, which that number would decrease at about 165 total later in deployment. We were shown our living arrangements and working quarters; there I would have discovered my passion for writing in an office similar to an old wooden cabin. God came through like he said he would though many others did not see it the same way. We were assigned patrols and the ECP (Entry Control Point) and no outside missions. God came through because we never had to engage in a firefight. Casualties are the effects of war but this deployment had none but a couple of severe injuries.

I spent the most of my time writing to keep my head clear and a connection with God. Never could I stop believing, not after witnessing what God has done for me in my darkest of times. The trials unfortunately, did not avast as depression, work, and people taunted me. It is always the ones who have a strong connection with God who have the toughest job and responsibility. To live right is to perform accordingly with God's word and give accordingly as he gives unto you. I gave my best at times and other times I had given so much that it was not enough of me left to perform. Other times I just had to give what was left of me and think only of the cross.

During this deployment I have learned so many things and I have grown so much. God preserved my life so that I may give unto someone else, a life for a life. Live free and never regret what just happen, only learn from it and take what you can to better yourself. We waste time talking about all the bad when we could have spent that second talking about God and what he has done. That second we may never get back, but my life I have and I thank God for it. I thank God every day, without faith, I would never have made it thus far.

LIFE'S NOT PROMISED

As I gaze out into the world touched by God, I realized how corrupt and poison it has become. Life on earth has become highly overrated taking in considerations; the crimes and genocide that have spoiled the foundation of existence. People all over the world are in need of help; not a savior but more like judgment and punishment. Blood has never been so thick on streets, death appears to never have a name, and kids fall short reaching promising conclusions in their lives. There should be no sympathy for ignorance; others should not have to pay for our inequities and selfish acts of survival. This is not acceptable, nor is it ok. It is sad to know people are comfortable with the level of disaster and distress.

Churches are only concerned with profit and landscape rather than the abased hope falling among the congregation. Where has the Jesus in us gone, when will someone assist their neighbor reminding them of how important their survival is. Wars are being fought within this nation as we turn away purposely shielding our eyes from the true nature of society. I stand alone with only a purpose and nothing more. Knocking on heaven's door until blood covers my knuckles. Alone camping outside until my need has been met by the only man able to relieve the pain. Families have turned on family spilling unnecessary blood like dogs. Evil has centralized into our homes and children as they are feed false hopes and assurance. The great words of Christ no longer contain the power it once had years ago, could death be the sentence for these heinous crimes and discriminate acts of instinct.

Heaven knows and heaven watches patiently waiting for God to claim the house once bestowed with peace and prosperity; patiently waiting for restoration. The God I serve deserves more than this abhorrent and conscientious place. No man deserves the conscious awareness of life, no commitment and desire to rebuild a kingdom for Christ but the undivided concentration into preparing a home for the omen eagerly submerging from the pits of hell. Songs of alcohol and sex abused the privilege of our voices God so kindly gave us. Preachers criticize and stereotype instead of exposing God for the phenomenal movement throughout this nation; falling apart, centralizing the negative habits into schools, neighborhoods, homes, and economically established businesses. Children becoming parents and parents purposely isolated, fathers killing the spirit of a man, worrier for God. Bread of life has molded and is no longer healthy to subdue the sin filled nature of man. Where has the Jesus in us gone?

I STAND ALONE

I stand alone tasting my own blood as I drift off to sleep, the next meal will be the bitter taste of defeat; what ironies to die like an animal and not man. I feel pain for the last time, lasting shame as light beams, forcing my eyes shut. This world could not have been a place for a king and his riches and glory. Breaking from the life and its existence I slumber deep to sleep. Tonight I dream of God, of angels, and of death. Take me with you and leave my corps behind for I have no use of it now. Fighting the good fight isolated me, emotional moment leading me up to the gates of heaven. There is nothing I can do at this point than here the heart beat slowly and unsteady. A band that has no talent on the instruments, speak to me the soul of one who condemned me. The pearly gates stand tall in front of me now, as I watch in awe.

I stand alone without friends and family, without materialistic possessions, and without sin. The world has one less child to take wonders in for I slumber and to never wake. My eyes have seen what all men have eagerly taunted so long to see. I find myself inside at the gates alone and confused. Cold tears fall down my face like a leaky faucet as I slowly progress forward among the dense clouds and frustration. Has the sky fallen, have I fallen too far asleep, inaudible and isolated I stand alone contempt.

WHERE THE BRIGHT THINGS ARE!

The fans are ecstatic, roaring like lions shaking the stadium. As I prepare for the walk of my life down to the ring feeling a slight taste of nausea and weakness in my knees. Time has never been so unbarring, the anticipation is killing me. Even the fans as far-fetched they were, reinvented the moments history already dealt; standing and cheering on the arrival of legends in which built the blood, sweat, and tears that helped make this business what it is today. Brocken bones and torn lindens was nothing more than just risk taking and acting upon instinct. A paycheck is a paycheck but here in this arena, it was like gold, every move precise and executed with proficiency. Flickers that are made by cameras fluttered the seats capturing monumental footage. This is where it all begins; maybe the end for some who at the match conclusion provoke standing ovations but the reality that just for one moment, any superstar can become an immortal. For one moment, life begins to question ones resilience and dedication and courage. This is not just any talk show you see on television, or some movie that sells millions of dollars at the box-office. This was "Wrestlemania", the showcase of the immortals where thousands in attendance and millions around the world watch at home. I take a moment backstage before Showtime and spell out the declaration. The declaration established when I first came to the World Wrestling Entertainment (WWE). What it means to be consistent, and maintain accuracy and control; the resistance and dedication boiling in my blood imprisoning fear. This time I will take the walk long awaited and overdue. This time I am willing to work.

The fans scream, chanting, and holding up signs of all sizes and colors. Chants of my name echoed throughout the stadium, as the beat of my music plays over the large screen. Slowly walking out from behind stage…

PRAISE YOU IN THIS STORM

Father, it's been so long since I've last written you. I just don't know where to start; so many things worth getting off my chest but seems like no use. I'm fighting a war both physically and mentally trying to conquer thoughts and... man. Feeling up the devil's pond knowing wrong from right but still I fall victim to so much. Worrying about what people say rather than what they do, it's just not me father. This isn't the way I was raised; this isn't the way I was taught. Who am I father is a mystery even to me; searching for answers I get lost and fall so deep within myself that I lose the way. My road is so broken that walking it would be impossible even with wings. Father help me, here my cry in this storm no matter how deep I may fall.

My heart is torn and cannot be restored, I feel like I have failed you putting life's problems before the cross. I raise my hands but sometimes don't mean it, what's the use when there's nothing to reach for. I know I sound vain but it's the truth. People threaten my success and even life, calling me out. Your blood keeps me safe but not all the time, I stretch your power week by week. I sing songs that soon lose their love and meaning. Poor, but still think rich among the wealthy though I have not yet made it; feels like there is something out there with my name on it. How can I carry on if I can't find you lord, how can I live if I can't breathe? How can I see ahead through this storm? Every time I raise my hands tears fall down my face knowing nothing will happen at that moment to change my situation. Devastation wrecks my life and even home, no lesson learned but the scars everlasting and openly displayed for others to see. God to be honest I can neither picture nor see your face, I cannot feel your touch...I don't hear your voice. When, where, and how. My hands covered with labor and blood, nothing more.

I turn off the TV because it's just nothing but more problems worse than mine. Lord, educate my mind and build my spirit, many days I've waited and still no answer. The only way I feel connected is if I write, write until something happens. Even if nothing does....I'll continue to praise you through this storm. I will continue to move up and down mountains, crawl and tumble. I'll praise you in this storm. So many days pass me by, leaving nothing but the residue of fear that soon I would be swallowed by this storm.

RECORD STORE DEAL

A kid and his mother walk into a record store one even. The two walk over to a collection of Christian music stacked neatly on a shelf towards the end of the store. The mother picks up a C.D, then cycles through the list of songs on the back, while the boy wonders off back towards the entrance of the store. As the mother becomes distracted looking at the collections still walking around the store, she does not realize the fact her son is no longer at her side. The little boy gazes out the window to see a tall man selling comic books across the streets. The boy as artistic as he was exits the door then slowly make his way to the edge of the curve where he was met with people shoving, running, yelling, and fussing; never noticing the boy as they walk by continuing on with their lives as if the he were a ghost. As the mother soon notices her child is missing she quickly drops the records from her hand then began scavenging around the store. Fearing the worst, holding back tears hoping her child would be sitting on the floor in one of the isles in the store.

Exhausting every effort searching she yells his name and panics questioning everyone in the store including the owner who just happened to be standing next to the cashier. No one could help the women nor recollect neither her nor the kid entering the store. She begins to cry glancing outside the window to see her child in the middle of the street with heavy traffic swarming on each side of him. Dashing out the door screaming the boy's name she knocks over a pedestrian who was walking by licking an ice cream cone. Cursing at the lady he gets up then walks off dusting the residue from off his jeans. After the lady gets to her feet she notices the boy has disappeared. Running down the street trying to get a glimpse at what could be left of her child, as everyone passed her by whispering and pointing amongst each other, some where even laughing at how ridiculous she looked with ice cream and sprinkles running down the side of her face. She reached the end of the block, there was nothing not even a clue of her son. She screams falling to her knees asking God for help, as people continue to pass her by consistently whispering amongst each other. What could she do what could she say, it wasn't like losing a pet or a dog; but her son? She began to feel comfort as a man touched her on the shoulder.

"What's the matter ma'am"?

A tall man said looking down at the woman. She stared up at his long bearded face for a moment then slowly spoke,

"My…my son is missing and I can't find him".

The tall man rubbed his beard then pointed in front of them,

"That wouldn't happen to be him standing over there by those comic books would it"?

The man said as she looked over to surely see her son reading comics across the street.

She runs over to him hugging the boy tightly in her arms thanking God for saving him.

"I'm sorry mommy",

WHAT GOD SEES IN ME

I would like to tell you about a kid who had nothing, knowing one day he would. Only time could tell when he would sprout wings and build a foundation that would shake the very grounds he walked; having an abundance of dreams and even visions of a world without fear, guilt, or sin. A world shy from perfect and split side of tranquility, people who never quench at public speaking on behave themselves, a world where homosexuality, addictions, racist, skepticism, and hypocrites are no more. As one we are accounted for and as one we answer to the highest calling. This kid feeling shy and confused of the power and destiny permanently etched in his path, begin to run, fearing that no one would accept such a gift, getting spat on, and thrown from off grace. We watch too much television that we can't see that God is within the smallest of creatures, we judge who is bad and good instead of the designed plan of God, scorn people for speaking out on behalf themselves when we won't praise God openly amongst one another. For every bad seed that is planted, it multiplies and gets worse. As children of God, stand out of Jesus way and let him do his job; remember he died alone. Preachers no longer preach but judging, forcing people to flee the church. Mothers giving up when it is as simple as acceptance and love, feel not afraid and be assured that even while you sleep God is hard at work. We turned life into boundaries and limitations when it is clearly a gift, a gift to watch the ocean dance, the sun giving light to the skies, and the trees lifting their branches in praise. Life has no meaning but the meaning define by God, we make our own rules and expect people to follow them; every decade more unjust. Even though this little kid follows God, still the doubts and confusion of even his own beliefs unfold.

As small as he was knowing that someday he would be the cause of a life dedicated to following Christ nothing more. To him, life was more than having the love of you always wanted, money you never had, or a dream coming to past. Life is meant as a gift, and to appreciate this gift the least we can do is treat God with undivided phenomenal love. Realize how precious life is and how every opportunity is a time to praise and thank God for his Gifts. Understand that being purposed is never bad. is nothing . Our purpose obviously is undefined for reasons why we have yet to ask the creator and the giver of life. Going to church is a blessing, keeping in mind the fact that not all churches know God. Some of us are so close to God, going to church just makes you stand out like a rose in a sunflower patch. We all grow differently and we all can't expect to be the same, God loves us for being ourselves. He sees nothing but the best in me, he sees me for who I am...

THE BENEDICTION

A long time ago, God gave me a vision seen only through the eyes of kings. My plan was vague and still remains a mystery even to me. Removing all that I am and replacing my very soul with that of a nation being held together by love, wisdom, courage, and prosperity. Not long have I discovered the power flowing within the depths of my veins, that one day "after life" it will be clear of my consistent sojourn side by side with God. Time after time doing the unthinkable, performing miracles, and out stepping the very grounds my Lord and savior Jesus Christ so passionately traveled. No, I'm not saying I'm perfect nor am I close to it; what makes man different from God is the truth; the truth that we are weak, we are small, and we are human. In my last dialogue, I addressed several issues of this world today and the fear being centralized among those who hide themselves from the truth, such people including myself, which I am not ashamed to say; have spent their entire lives living in lies, in fear, causing an uprising and possibly a war leading to a blank solution.

Purposely, I am writing this to insure you that in time all shall confess and be charged. Though I am far away from home, I am not far away from God. Let us end this war and join together, no matter where we may come from. Let the elaborate ways of people be exposed not drowned along with dreams. Jesus stepping out into the world was met with animosity and accused for being different. People step out every day and are met with this same mentality. I sadly witness a family charging their own child of sin and being a backslider; being forced to live either by their rules or perish alone in darkness. Who are we to keep a child from his or her character birthed by God? Life is a gift, and not a right; I chose to not blend in but step out along with Jesus. Take life and all the miracles in God's hands with it, stay alive and fight, bringing down the walls of freedom and let it flood nothing but God's riches and glory. Happiness may be just a smile away, give life to someone who may be going through. Smile and tell them God loves you, smile and remind them of love that once had a home in their hearts. I love you and pray for nothing but the best, for it is yet to come.

VALUES OF LIFE

Sacrifice after sacrifice, seems as though putting life on the line and in return I receive jewels of less value. My labor in life has neither meaning nor reward, stuck with fortunate circumstances and a divided personality; cold yet still manage to keep warm somehow each day. The taste of failure makes me gag, feeling as if I have no purpose. My career frets me, pondering if I have a chance to make it slowly but steadily pulling through. It is a gift to know happiness, for a short time the future is clear but remains in disarray. Pieces of promised accomplishments lead the worshippers to victory, but parish by demons prompted by irrelevant misfortunes. Through this dark and abandon tunnel shall I rise along with Abraham and claim all that in which is separated from me; scratch and claw the very existence of my being openly for all to see.

Nothing to hide if there is nothing to show, only the weak minded life walks behind the cross instead of in front. Victory cushions the blow of silence; in reality failure has no remorse for the broken, dealing a blind hand. The game is resilience, in conclusion determined by outperforming predicted outcomes of self elevation. Also keep in mind the preparation involved during rehabilitation. I shall fall not, for God invested the strength of a nation in me. To live a dream according to this psalm is to live flawlessly without hesitation and worry. To glide along the coattails of both freedom and prosperity; to fly without having wings. I walk off the edge and never think twice believing faith will supply the following step. Though shall not test God, be as it may God will be pleased of faith in analogy with his word. Let victory poor down like raining water both spiritually and mentally filling every significant need. Rise with humanity and become stable like trees.

YOU'RE NOT ALONE

The storm has come to claim everything in your life; it has come to finally end your existence. You call on God and get no answer time after time. Even while it rains pours down on you like never before, you cling to your pride and question if this is the way. Lover after lover, friend after friend, nothing seems to go right in this debilitating life. Work is little if not at all while taking care of a young growing child as he cries at times because he too is hungry and cold. The pain on his face while you try to explain the circumstances forge a smile upon yours, knowing everything won't be just fine. Plans that you've made have fallen along with the ounce of faith which once settled strongly in your heart. Even if you cry all night you will get through, soon there will be a break through flooding the door of heaven with your tears. God knows and understands; he too weeps over your situation and waits for your hand not your towel. Once in a while we all go through storms that take up most our lives, sometimes causing dreams to be delayed and faith to subside.

We change everything about ourselves and even go as far as changing the way we communicate with others. Building a wall stacked with sadness, misery, and depression. Submerged in fear and clinging on to hope, hope that somehow someway you'll get through. Say that you're not afraid and that you've got things sorted out. "This is it", you say as you walk into another broken story. Hold on to what is left of God in your heart, hold on and never think God cannot see or understand. Headstrong yet still doubting your decisions and eventually began to doubt God. You're not alone; it is so easy to say "I've made it" when physically seeing such an accomplishment is impossible in your state. The race seems too long and you fall out to the side before attempting to run. No one cares about your pain, no one knows of your situation; you're not alone. Taking pills, cutting, self abuse…you're not alone. I realized how great God was after my sins were forgiven, my kidneys were healed, backsliding had been forgotten, and I've made it this far. Sometimes it's not about how bad your situation is, but how good things are in the storm. I've been scared before and even lost my way countless times, at one point doubting God had even existed.

It is good to know God on your own instead of what everyone else says, miracles performed in your life may not make since to everyone else. Just give God a chance, bring down your wall and smile. Speak of good wonders and not of bad intentions. Talk to God when you're alone, even when it feels awkward. You are not alone.

KIMBLE PSALM

God, my healer, protector, and giver of life promised me two things; happiness and victory. Though at the time I was just a kid and did not understand the full potential and circumstances, it was clear that a calling had taken place. I walked towards God's words and promises with a straight edge mind and dedication in my heart. To walk with God, one must master faith and understand to a degree the importance of a partnership. Faith could have been the only substitute for hope when in times of crisis, I recall leaning on heaven's door night and day for answers and relief from both people and situations. Though the bible tells us many things, it will take a spiritual connectivity with God in order to understand the true meaning of the principles and keys in order to reach a level of competence. Higher learning will take affect once you accept what is given unto you by God, recognizing the calling on your life.

The longest storm thus far remains evident in my life even when it has blown away. I had to have gone through something in order to get somewhere, like all things progress takes effect upon self acceptance to take on what is before you. I chosen to endure things and accept God's will for he knows what is best, countervailing if it may be too adhesive or more than you can bear. God favored me for one reason, faith. Without faith, I would have fallen or lost my way some time ago. Family, friends, and possessions shook my beliefs, causing questions to uproot spontaneously in which lowered me into denial and into a backsliding mentality. Yes, time has an effect on everyone and is the crucial way of living. I found myself attempting to outthink God as if I were in control and God just played as a watcher, subsequently I slipped deep into depression and eventually claiming suicide. Sadly submitting to suicide two times, the last time God spoke to me shaking the very grounds I walked responding

"I need you to survive".

Free from depression, heartache, pain, and sin I stand today. Words are just puppets but somehow if understood it makes music, soft and angelic sounds that soothe the spirit; which is why music has been my soul quencher in those hard times, to listen and concentrate and feel angels surround me, singing, dancing, and rejoicing as I did. We are only human and have phobias that interfere with the ability to socialize, work, or go about our everyday lives. God takes those fears and raps them around you, to draw you close, and understand that he has even those things that hurt us in his hands. The greatest laws I try to teach is go ahead and be yourself, being ashamed of who you are is not healthy to your mind. Yes, God wants to give you a chance at life, but not to believe you're a bad seed. All things grow differently and learn diversely like children, I call this "free", meaning free from everything and anything that may try to break or destroy the luminous people we are. Smile and walk with pride for you are favored; I spent my entire life wondering if I made God proud when it was clear all along, I'm still here. I even went as far as changing myself and ways, believing I could never be accepted by people. Today I live free and with so much happiness, friends come and go but God never shift change. They may say whatever they want, treat me as heinously as they know how, but I'll still be here. Thankfully love keeps me close and in great shape, and I shall follow God all the days of my life.

AN ANGEL NAMED IRENE

While down one day on my hands and knees in prayer, the back door to the kitchen flew open as if someone had pushed it forcefully. The winds can get a little rough in Kansas especially around this time of year. Startled and slightly hesitant, I stood to my feet but slowly as the blood rushed down my legs. This was an every night ritual that would soothe me at least for a while, but I knew that it wouldn't take long until the darkness would come to claim me once again. As I shut and locked the back door a chill breeze came rushing in and swarmed around the kitchen, clinging pops and pans knocking towels onto the parquet floor; making a whistle which sounded like a hymn as it blew by, from the kitchen to my bedroom and from my bedroom to the living room. Shortly after I had cleaned up the mess left behind, I heard a soft sound coming from the same place in which the winds had settled. From the hall I could see a shadow prancing about in the living room, dancing to be exact as the sweet sounds continued to play. I couldn't make it out, what was there is a mystery even today. I stood there in the middle of the hall just watching the shadow and listening to the sounds coming from that same place, never wanting to know what was going on but just wanted to take in all the happiness and peace that swarmed around me.

After about 2-3 minutes or so I was able to move, falling to the floor in tears. I just lay their as huge blobs fell down my face; the funny thing is that with every drop I felt more and more relieved. In my 50 years of living, I've never felt so young, pure, and so happy. The fact of the matter is, this old body could just as well give up and I may be on my way home. This different and odd aroma came over me and I couldn't breathe. It was as if submerged in a pool of mud, by the time I got strength to lift my head the shadow had disappeared and the music stopped. What could explain what just happened in my house? All alone, no witnesses which gives me a great story to tell during tea time if I can make it till then.

Quickly I sat up, smiling and lifting my hands towards heaven shouting in an unusual tongue. Though my ears could not interpret, my mind understood every word as if this was my native tongue. No more tears, my legs felt relieved from arthritis, the heart pains I complained about were not there anymore, problem after problem and cure after cure I began to notice. Standing to my feet dancing and continuing to shout in the same unusual tongue, although there was no music I made my own. Singing and dancing about from the hall and eventually into the living room to settle down on the sofa. Consistently telling myself to never stop, don't quit, and continue to dance not resting for too long shooting back up to my feet. Dancing until the sun ruled the skies, and dancing even more until I've reached the 12th hour mark. For an old woman it is not common to dance like that, but I did not notice the time nor did I consider the fact I have been dancing for so long. I recall how bright things were in the room, it was really impossible and unbearable; all I could see is those things in which were just plain black and even still I could only see them slightly.

After I had retired from dancing, I hit the floor in the same way I had earlier. Although there were no tears, the pains in which I once felt suddenly came rushing back all at once; an old woman once again, helpless lying on the floor as if about to die. I could feel so much tension in my legs that standing would be impossible without substantial amount of pain. The headache centralized from the temple to the center of my head and down to the ears. My shoulders, arms, and even back felt like stab wombs to every inch of flesh. Yes, I'm in worse shape than before, crawling to the phone I managed to grab a hold of the cord and yank until the receiver fell in my hands. Even to dial 9.1.1. was a huge accomplishment in my state of health. It was either dial or die. I don't know why I just didn't chose to die for I truly believe that heaven had landed in my home that day.

After being released from the hospital, my story about how heaven came to my home was unbelievable to some people. Doctors stated I was having a heart attack right before I had called and that explains the mythical phase I was going through. Others say that the angel Irene visited me and brought a little piece of heaven down with her, but whatever it may be I know that one day I will feel that same feeling I had once before I landed myself in the emergency room. I know that heaven is real and all those things that make us happy are nothing compared to praising God and living with him. Peace, love, happiness, and life had never felt so good to me now that I'm reaching my 61st birthday. I just hope that one day the angel Irene would stumble upon you so that you can feel what I have felt, see what I have seen, and taste nothing but sweet honey. I always sit and long for that moment again, even if I would have to endure pain once again. It would be worth it.

GOD FAVORED ME

Taken from the higher place, and abased to a much lower position, torn yet still I stand. Forgotten and abandoned but not for looks, for I am characterized by judgmental and averted friends. Still breathing, heart beating; I charge without a care of lost favor once felt. I know that God had an amazing hand stretched forward over me with favor. Bruise my body, killed my spirit, and spat on my gifts of labor. Friends showed up and left the same day laughing and pointing at all my mistakes. The gift of life has been abused by both sides, sadly I have attempted to end it twice, but God favored me because I'm still here. My enemies never gave up and tried even harder, given the fact I am favored and never put aside. Belated, I stand happy to carry a cross symbolizing what was given back to me.

No longer do I cry tears of remorse but feel an ocean overflowing the gates of heaven to rain down on the seeds that have been planted in favor of me. I'm here with just a testimony and how God favored me, deeply in the roots of my heart lays a light burning sufficiently enough for others to see the favor on my life. I claim victory, prosperity, an overflowing caring love, and a rich foundation congested of favor. In the past my life was felt as shy and wooden built, torn, shattered, and swallowed by the dark forebode. With favor from God the dark days are over, my foundation is built of pure gold, no more sad songs of absolute havoc, for this time I play a special instrument of praise and more suitable to my character.

To listen to God's ground-shaking voice and feel his glorious presents and all so favorable touch is worth the trials, tears, and sacrifice. God favors me…

FREE

Free to be the person God created me to be; free to dance, love, and speak. I am free to express myself in any and every way, for it is me who can change adaptation, evolution, and resolution. I am the face of many and swag of only one. The definition of resilience and the color of life, I am free and never held in captivity. Free to be me; wings of an angel, fight of a lord, and strength of a storm. I am simple yet sweet with a hint of spice; great at anything and better at more. My voice has no limitations, and is always wanted. Only kings desire such exquisite character and important enough Jesus would die for. I am free to be me...

LORD OF WAR

Fear…never tasted so good, the evil rising amongst us has nothing on a warrior; trained and proficient in tactics of great pain. To hear them cry as I show them pieces of their own flesh, and to hear them beg like debilitated slaves in the presents of me…Lord of War. Mercy has not a breath to spare as my sword drinks from the blood of those so called opponents. It is said no man can escape his own destiny and that he will submit to his analogy, this I have no approval for they submit to me. I fight with pride, resilience, consistence, and with damnation on my mind. I have no heart to forgive or to forget, it behooves those who oppose me never to avast. The ironsmith, the creator of redemption; their souls soothes the hunger in my heart. Some say I am the Grim Reaper and others say I am the advocate for both good and evil, for it does not matter what title I am given it is relevant death rides my veins.

Lord of War, enemy of enemies, I am the best in what I do, pleasuring my sick and innovative mind vanquishing without a care. One by one they have come to claim what God himself kindly dealt me, but one by one they all have tasted the bitter end of defeat attempting to end my life. I scorn at the weak and laugh at the dead, no man can match my strength and excellence. Surely I say to you, be aware of where you fall…it will be your last. The Lord of War has risen and I plan not to sleep until I have had my fill of blood…of souls. My record is unmatched and uncanny; to prevail and never kneel has been my creed. To go home with hands congested of limbs and a nation of casualties in my name placed me above the chain of command. They fear me; run when someone speaks of my name, and even bring gifts to my door for protection. The Lord of War and of death has no side, no remorse, and no mercy. The Lord of War is within me…

VICTORY

Long overdue and long awaited I stand, filled and restored. God came through when it was mentally and physically unbarring; at the end. Standing there with his arms wide open and an enormous smile crafted so heartwarming upon his face. On this day I claim victory, prosperity, and growth. I declare freedom in its most highest of forms; dealt nothing but the best my enemies could throw at me and still I stand, unbroken, and unmoved. I put self aside just too at least grab hold of my savior's gown and even be dragged into a new declaration. The cross I could not bear, but the trials and tribulations I could stand only for so long. Suicide, depression, poverty, and diversions I bind up in the name of Jesus; break and fold those entering my stronghold and I ask that a shower of blessings to govern me. Praise be the name of all things living and non living, I will exult your name at all times never missing a beat.

For my life has been paid in full, walking free and deeply in love with the one who has given me victory. Triumph has started my new season and love has embellished the contents of its nature, I have a new song in which I can sing thankfully victory. The enemy may come and go as he please nor at any time may I fret or show debilitation. I am the reason evil works so hard and even harder when I resist,

I am the annoying light in their darkest pit, I am a seed that has been planted and I refuse to move. Water runs down stream but I swim up it, no time to avast for I have a meeting with Christ at the end of this trail. You can't hold me down but only speak and only when spoken too. My enemies can't handle me therefore giving up only to come back later for the same results; a game of everlasting life.

My lord requests me again, and this time I am happy to accommodate for I am better, wiser, and stronger, anxiously grabbing my wings and racing towards God's voice. Rewarded, restored, and redeemed; Jesus is my hero for whom I live and breathe. I could have lost my way and given up but I held on; power to cross over and claim what is rightfully mine, love to endure and withstand friends who turn away, courage when in times of abased faith stand in the midst of a crowd and cry out the name of Jesus, finally faith, to trust and allow God to drive me above and beyond man's expectations. I'm still here, still standing and walking along side Christ with my own stone, ready for that day when I am able to cast it away. The lord has spoke to me and has guaranteed and assured me of peace, and victory. I am a walking testimony of so many stories, of a road touched by more people like myself. Hold on my brother my sister; help is on the way for God's promises are real.

STRENGTH PRAYER

God I'm more than a conqueror, with favor from you Lord my trials and tribulations will last till morning; for I speak joy in which soon will come. Protect my heart and guide only my mind, let my spirit do the talking. In times of crisis father, I am reminded of the cross, for strength and encouragement that I cannot get from friends or family. Father I lean on your word and I know at times I must travel alone, I beg you father never allow me to travel far, never allow me to stay down. I look up to the skies and I feel your presents, even when held in captivity by those who conspire against me. Lord when I couldn't do for myself you did for me, lord when the rain wouldn't stop pouring you sent someone to my aid. I found favor and comfort in the most strange ways, broken relationships, fake friends, denial, and even sickness and health.

Lord I ask for forgiveness and mercy on my sinful ways. Weak but I am maid strong, doubtful but I lean on faith, impatient but I will walk and not faint. God I shutter and close my door to unfamiliar folks, I pray that I am open and sincere. Lord I speak life and not of death. At times I hurt so badly but favor suffices me for a while, they may never know what I am going through father. My hands trembles, my legs are weak, my heart aches, and I am pushed to the edge physically and mentally day by day, but to know that victory comes in the morning comforts the most phenomenal and unbarring pains. I will not look back father but only learn from my mistakes and ask for forgiveness. Lord I say yes to your will without hesitation, I know that one day you'll say yes for my soul as I take my rightful place in heaven. God I know my marriage will be justified, peace filled, and with great favor. Lord when I fill it is getting better it gets worse, you promised bad days in which make me stronger, better, wiser and a more valuable asset to your kingdom and a threat to my enemy.

Lord I fall at your feet to be washed from drug abuse and mishaps. I am a child of Christ and doer of your all so mighty word. Praise kept me when the well was dry; Lord you continue to sit with me even when I turned away.

CONFESSIONS OF A SINNER

Sometimes I feel like there is no way out of this stronghold, bending over backwards to help those who in return spit in my face. When I cry and lift my hands it is only the person inside that understands the deepest sadness that governs me. My pastor says God is the way and he will supply all of your needs, but how can God make anything out of this disaster and where could I possibly be after this storm. Will there ever be a change? For so long I've sat in the back of church pretending to listen, watching others rejoice. What could they possibly have that makes them so happy, what gives them the right? I have been called so many things and put on the spot as an idol for evil and wickedness. Could I pray for you? No leave me alone, nothing ever happens. I wonder why God allows me to go through so much; people who have never accepted Christ are doing so much better than those who have.

The same story unfolds when others tell me to be strong, but I want to know when my time will come. I feel your pain, they say but fail to give me proof; I see no tears, nor do I see them holding the one spot that has been neglected, torn, and abused. I'm so tired of coming to church and leave in the same condition, what will it take to get help? Every time I leave church, I leave alone. When I step into my home, I am alone, and when I lay down, I am alone. No one cares as long as they are blessed in return for being good Samaritans. Open the bible and read Psalms 6:6, Mathews 27:7, or just read; will it take back all that I have been through? How can reading the bible give me a way out? I am ready to give up but feel there is a way, I just haven't found it. In those times when my bills are too high, my car has been towed, and someone close to me died, where was God. Was he just watching as the enemy invaded my home and took everything I ever had, including those things that used to keep me so close to the cross?

When I speak to God, I feel alone. Is there anyone there? I feel so embarrassed when people point and laugh catching me in those times. Why do you cry all the time, when will you just have faith and let God take care of your burdens? I have tried and feel no assurance, love, or restoration. My best friend decided to submit leaving this world behind, she says a heart was never meant for this type of punishment and abuse. Will there ever be a change? What can I say or do just for answers or even a touch? The man on the corner says life has no purpose or meaning, we are puppets created only to take up room on this earth. Why did that feel right? My choices in life are justified and respectful to God's expectations. What am I doing wrong? I confessed my sins and confronted the congregation years ago, why am I still standing here with the faint taste of that confession today. When will it end and will there ever be a change...
Yes, I know you have so many questions and just really want answers. Even though things are not as you would want them to be, God sees what you are going through. If he didn't care, he wouldn't have given us his only son. To allow you to go through so much is for a purpose and know that God has his hands all over your situation. There will be a conclusion to this storm. Allow God to hold you through those nights, welcome him in

BAD DAYS (SONG)

I've had my… bad days… I've had… my sad days… had so many… ups and downs, cried everyday and never smiled… through it all… I kept my faith, in God… above… and I'm happy to say my bad days are gone… my friends turned and walked away…I almost gave but I kept the faith…my trials lasted, far more nights than days… God stepped in and saved the day… through it all… I kept my faith, in God… above… and I'm happy… to say my bad days are gone…yes I'm happy… to say my bad days are gone…

In the end I can say…the darkness… didn't stay…with faith and trust in God… I'm able to step out away from all… my God held me in his arms… and kept me safe from all harm…but I tell you, through it all… I kept my faith, in God… above… and I'm happy… to say my bad days are gone… through it all… I kept my faith, in God… above… and I'm happy… to say my bad days are gone… yeah I'm happy… to say my bad days are gone…yes I'm happy… to say my bad days are gone…I'm happy…to say… my bad days…are gone…

MELODY (SONG)

You carried… me… through my… storm… and when in doubt… you guided me for so… long… for that I say… thank you…thank you… thank you. Thank you…thank you… thank you…finally… I've made… it through… and now I see…I never would have made it… without… you… and I say… thank you…thank you… thank you… thank you…thank you… thank you…when I fall… it was you… who seen me through… so thank you…thank you… thank you… thank you Jesus